WORDS · CHORDS · M

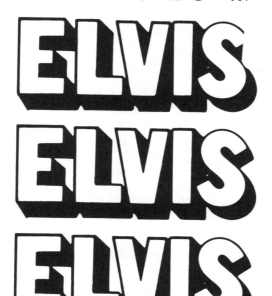

ELVIS ELVIS ELVIS

100 GREATEST HITS

This publication is not for sale in
the E.C. and/or Australia
or New Zealand.

HAL•LEONARD™
CORPORATION
7777 W. BLUEMOUND RD. P.O. BOX 13819 MILWAUKEE, WI 53213

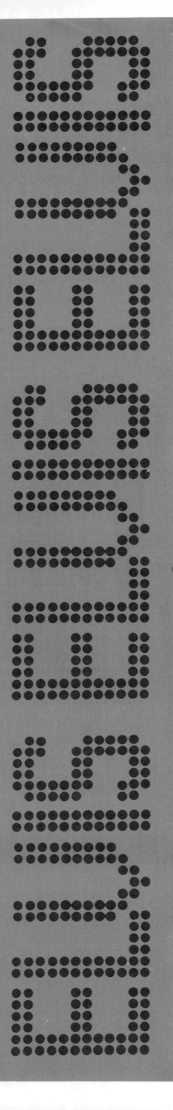

Contents

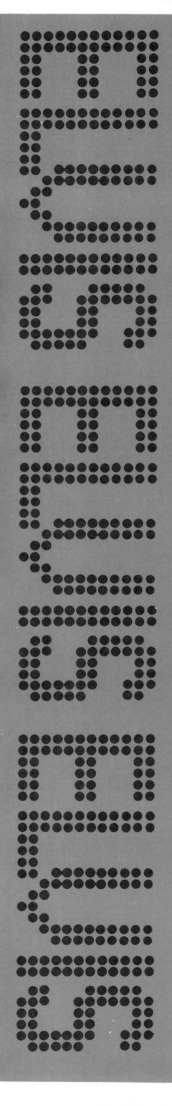

BLUE SUEDE SHOES

Words and Music by
CARL LEE PERKINS

130-00721
1587

1587

BLUE GUITAR

Words and Music by
SHEB WOOLEY

BLUE MOON

Lyric by
LORENZ HART

Music by
RICHARD RODGERS

CAN'T HELP FALLING IN LOVE

Words and Music by
GEORGE WEISS
HUGO PERETTI
LUIGI CREATORE

146-00997
1587

ALL SHOOK UP

By
OTIS BLACKWELL
and ELVIS PRESLEY

Medium Shuffle Rhythm

A-well-a, bless my soul, What's wrong with me?__ I'm itch-ing like a man__ on a

fuz-zy tree__ My friends say I'm act-in' queer as a bug__ I'm in love I'm

ALL SHOOK UP!__ Mm__ mm oh, oh, yeah,__ yeah!_____ My

1587

hands are sha-ky and my knees are weak,__ I can't seem to stand__ on my

own two feet,__ Who do you thank when you have such luck? I'm in love! I'm

ALL SHOOK UP!__ Mm__ mm oh, oh, yeah,__ yeah!_____

1. Please don't ask what's on my mind,_I'm a lit-tle mixed up but I'm feel-in' fine._When I'm
2. Tongue gets tied when I try to speak, My__ in-sides shake like a leaf on a tree,_There's

Opt.

near_ that girl that_ I_ love best, My_ heart beats so it scares_me to death!
on-ly one cure for this soul_ of mine, That's to have the girl that I love_ so_ fine! } She

G. I. BLUES

Words and Music by
SID TEPPER
ROY C. BENNETT

Verse

1. They give us a room with a view of the beau-ti-ful Rhine.
2. (We) get has-sen-fef-fer and black pump-er-nick-el for chow.
3. (We'd) like to be he-roes, but all that we do here is march.
4. (The) Frau-leins are pret-ty as flow'rs, but we can't make a pass.

They give us a room with a view of the beau-ti-ful
We get has-sen-fef-fer and black pump-er-nick-el for
We'd like to be he-roes, but all that we do here is
The Frau-leins are pret-ty as flow'rs, but we can't make a

Rhine. Gim-me a mud-dy old creek in
chow. I'd blow my next month's pay for a
march. And they don't give the Pur-ple
pass. 'Cause they're all wear-in' signs say-in',

146-04510
1587

Tex - as   an - y   old   time.
slice   of   Tex - as   cow.
Heart   for   a   fall - en   arch.
"Keep - en Sie   off ___ the   grass!"

Chorus

I've got those hup, two, three, four, oc - cu - pa - tion G. I. Blues.

From my G. I. hair to the heels of my G. I. shoes.

(Tacet)

And if I don't go state - side ___ soon, I'm gon - na blow my

(Tacet)

fuse.

2. We
3. We'd
4. The

fuse. _____

HEARTBREAK HOTEL

By
MAE BOREN AXTON
TOMMY DURDEN
and ELVIS PRESLEY

HOUND DOG

Words and Music by
JERRY LEIBER *and*
MIKE STOLLER

142-05595
1587

When they said you was high-classed, well, that was just a lie.

When they said you was high-classed; well, that was just a lie.

Well, ___ you ain't nev-er caught a rab-bit and you ain't no friend of

mine.

You ain't noth-in' but a mine.

I'M LEAVIN'

Words and Music by
MICHAEL JARRETT
and **SONNY CHARLES**

Moderately, with a beat

La, la, la, la, la, la, la, la, la, la, la, la, la.

La, la, la, la, la, la, la, la, la, la, la, la, la.

1. How will I know if I ar-rive in time to
2. Where will I go? Who will I have to lie be-

know you?
side me,

If you had tak-en the time to
to ease this emp-ti-ness in

I WANT YOU, I NEED YOU, I LOVE YOU

Words by
MAURICE MYSELS

Music by
IRA KOSLOFF

IT'S NOW OR NEVER

Words and Music by
AARON SCHROEDER
WALLY GOLD

Moderately

146-07169
1587

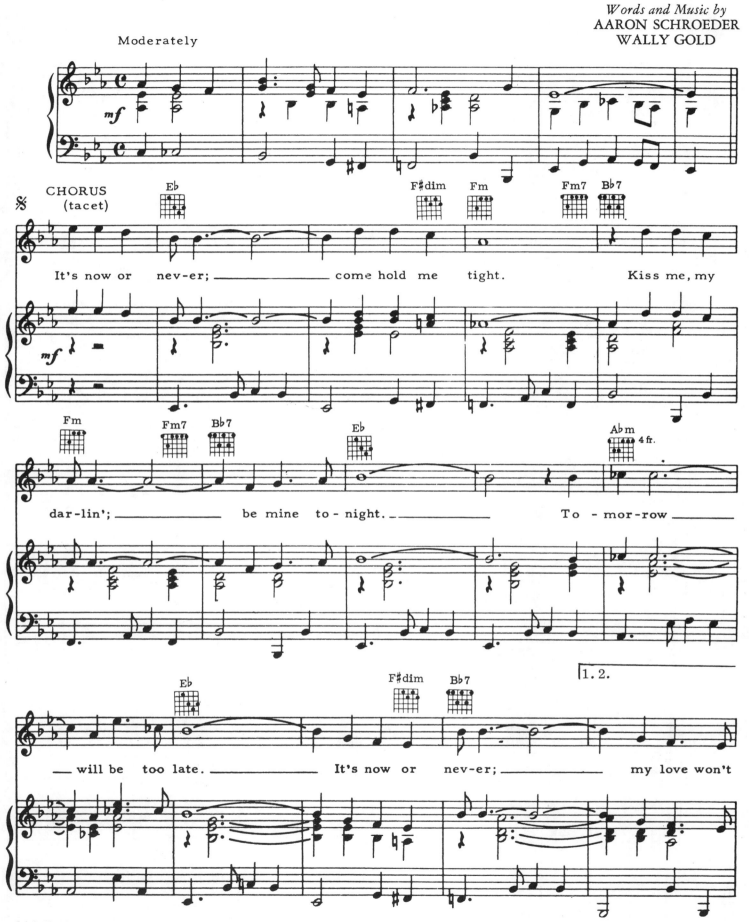

LOVE ME TENDER

Words and Music by
ELVIS PRESLEY and
VERA MATSON

Chorus

EXTRA VERSE

4. When at last my dreams come true,

Darling, this I know:

Happiness will follow you

Everywhere you go.

IT'S A MATTER OF TIME

Words and Music by
CLIVE WESTLAKE

ONLY BELIEVE

Words and Music by
PAUL RADER
ELVIS PRESLEY

JAILHOUSE ROCK

Words and Music by
JERRY LEIBER and
MIKE STOLLER

142-07288
1587

4. The sad sack was a-sittin' on a block of stone,
Way over in the corner weeping all alone.
The warden said: Hey, buddy, don't you be no square.
If you can't find a partner, use a wooden chair!
Let's rock, etc.

5. Shifty Henry said to Bugs: For Heaven's sake,
No one's lookin'; now's our chance to make a break.
Bugsy turned to Shifty and he said: Nix, nix;
I wanna stick around a while and get my kicks.
Let's rock, etc.

SEEING IS BELIEVING

Words by
BOBBY GENE WEST

Music by
BOBBY GENE WEST
and **GLEN SPREEN**

STUCK ON YOU

Words and Music by
AARON SCHROEDER
J. LESLIE McFARLAND

You can shake an ap - ple off an ap - ple tree._
Gon - na run my fin - gers thru your long black hair._

Shake-a shake-a, sug-ar, but you'll nev-er shake me._ Uh-uh-uh._
Squeeze_ you _ tight-er than a griz - zly bear.. Uh-huh-huh._

No-sir - ee,_ uh-uh. _ I'm gon - na
Yes-sir - ee,_ uh-huh. _ I'm gon - na

146-14886
1587

SURRENDER

Original Italian Lyrics by
G. B. DE CURTIS
Music by
E. DE CURTIS

English Words and Adaptation
By
DOC POMUS
MORT SHUMAN

48

1587

SUSPICIOUS MINDS

By
MARK JAMES

1587

1587

I FEEL THAT I'VE KNOWN YOU FOREVER

Words and Music by
DOC POMUS
ALAN JEFFREYS

142-05876
1587

YOU DON'T HAVE TO SAY YOU LOVE ME

Original Italian Lyrics by
V. PALLAVICINI
English Lyrics by
VICKI WICKHAM *and* **SIMON NAPIER-BELL**

Music by
P. DONAGGIO

1587

YOU'RE A HEARTBREAKER

Words and Music by
JACK SALLEE

AMAZING GRACE

By
ELVIS PRESLEY

1587

ANGEL

Words and Music by
SID TEPPER
ROY C. BENNETT

146-00200
1587

ANYPLACE IS PARADISE

Words and Music by
JOE THOMAS

CHORUS

1. Wheth-er I'm rid-ing down the high-way or
2. Wheth-er we're stand-ing on your door-step or

walk-ing down the street, It makes no dif-f'rence,ba-by doll,___ wher-
sit-ting in the park, Or stroll-ing down a shad-y lane ___ or

ev-er we chance to meet, Each time I hold your lit-tle hand,— it makes me
danc—ing in the dark, Where I can take you in my arms— and look in-

142-00244
1587

feel so ver- y nice.___ An - y -place is par - a - dise___ when I'm with
to your pret- ty eyes.___ An - y -place is par - a - dise___ when I'm with

1.

you. 2. Wheth-er we're

2.

you.

3. Give me a cave up in the mountains

  Or a shack down by the sea,

  And ı will be in heaven

  If I have you there with me,

  Where I can kiss your tender lips

  And see the heaven in your eyes.

  Anyplace is paradise

  When I'm with you.

4. Baby, I'd live deep in the jungle

  And sleep up in a tree,

  And let the rest of the world go by,

  If you were there with me,

  Where I could love you all the time;

  Baby, the jungle would be nice.

  Anyplace ıs paradise

  When I'm with you.

ALL THAT I AM

Words and Music by
SID TEPPER and
ROY C. BENNETT

Moderately Slow, Smoothly, and Tenderly

All that I am or ev - er hope to be lies in your hands. You are my des - ti - ny. When you are in my arms, I

68

1587

ANY WAY YOU WANT ME

(THAT'S HOW I WILL BE)

Words and Music by
AARON SCHROEDER
and *CLIFF OWENS*

69

AS LONG AS I HAVE YOU

Words by
FRED WISE

Music by
BEN WEISMAN

Chorus

Let the stars_ fade and fall_ and I won't_ care at all As long as I have you. Ev-'ry kiss_ brings a thrill_ and I know_ that it will As long as I have you. Let's

73

1587

BEGINNER'S LUCK

Words and Music by
SID TEPPER *and*
ROY C. BENNETT

Moderately, with feeling

First time I fell in love, I fell in love with you,

First time I dared to dream, my on-ly dream came true.

Must be be-gin-ner's luck to wish up-on a star, Then

o-pen up my eyes and there you are.

146-02196
1587

BIG BOOTS

Words by
SID WAYNE

Music by
SHERMAN EDWARDS

Music Box Effect

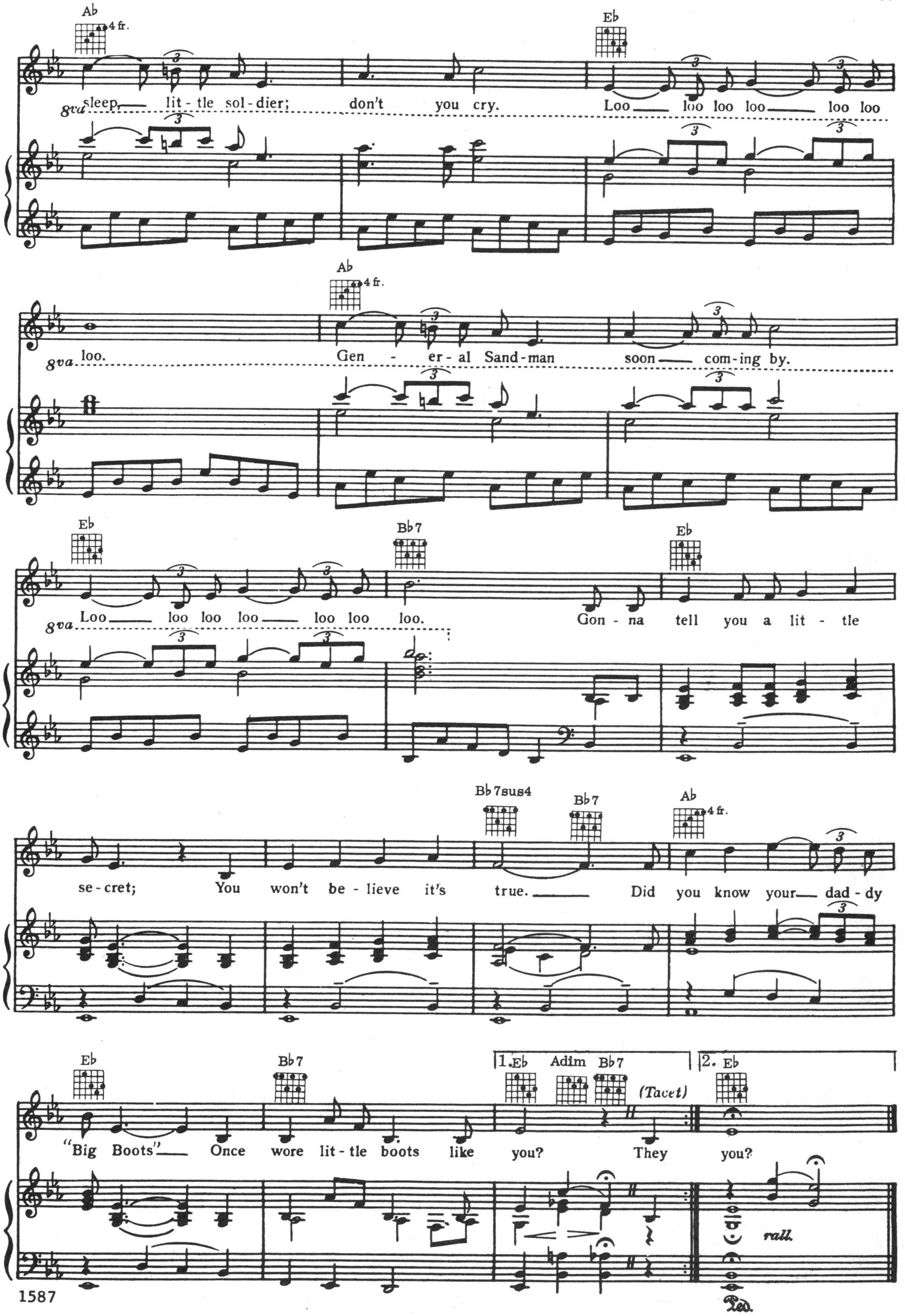

A BIG HUNK O' LOVE

Words and Music by
AARON SCHROEDER
SID WYCHE

142-00592
1587

79

1587

3. I got a wish-bone in my pock-et. I got a rab-bit's foot 'round my wrist. And I'd have

ev - 'ry-thing my luck-y charms could bring ___ if you gim-me just one sweet

kiss, oh, no no no no no no no, ba - by. I ain't ask-in' much of you.

Just a big-a big-a big-a hunk o' love will do. ___

DON'T LEAVE ME NOW

Words and Music by
AARON SCHROEDER
and **BEN WEISMAN**

A BOY LIKE ME, A GIRL LIKE YOU

Words and Music by
SID TEPPER
ROY C. BENNETT

CINDY, CINDY

Words and Music by
BUDDY KAYE, BEN WEISMAN
and D. FULLER

3. Need you in the mornin' to start the coffee pot,
   Need you in the afternoon, to fan me when I'm hot.
   Need you in the evenin' when supper time is thru,
   What I'm really tryin' to say is I can't get enough of you. .
   (Chorus)

4. If I were a musician, I'd harp on just one thing,
   You should never play my heart, the way you pluck a string.
   If only you would love me, sincerely tell me so,
   I'd beat the drums about you, baby, to let the whole world know.
   (Chorus)

COME ALONG

Words and Music by
DAVID HESS

With a Dixieland beat

Chorus

Come a - long, Come a - long, There's a full moon shin - in' bright. Come a - long, Come a - long, We're gon - na

{ hit Saint Lou - is } to - night.
{ win a for - tune }

Segue to Verse.

DO NOT DISTURB

Words and Music by
BILL GIANT
BERNIE BAUM *and*
FLORENCE KAYE

Moderately

1. Let's take the phone off the hook,
2. I'll — just pull down that blind,
3. Ev - 'ry - thing's right to - night,

Turn the amp 'way down low;   Ba - by, put down that
Now come o - ver here;   I got one thing in
Mm, it's great when we kiss;   Now your arms hold me

142-03424
1587

DON'T

Words and Music by
**JERRY LEIBER
MIKE STOLLER**

FRANKIE AND JOHNNIE

By
FRED KARGER
ALEX GOTTLIEB
and BEN WEISMAN

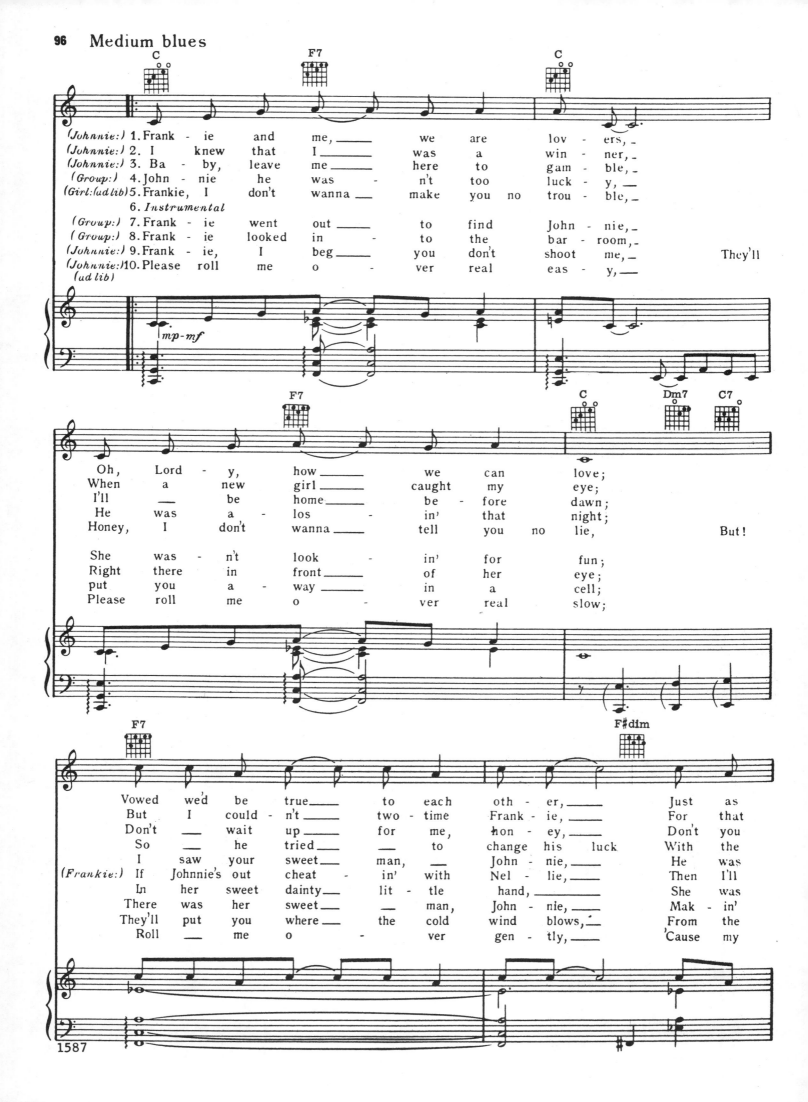

| C | G7 | Cdim | C | Am7 |

true as stars a - bove. — I'm your
chick as named Nel - lie Bly. I'm Frank - ie's
wor - ry while I'm gone. — *(Frankie:)* You're my
gal who was - n't right. He's Frank - ie's
messin' around with that Nellie Bly. Honey, he's your
have to do him in. 'Cause he's my
totin' a forty - four gun. To shoot her
love to Nel - lie Bly. He was her
hot - test corner of hell. — *(Frankie:)* Johnnie, you're my
wound it hurts me so. I was your

| G7 | Dm7 | G7 | | Ab7 | G7+5 | **1. to 9.** C | C7 | F | F#dim |

man, _____ I'll nev - er do ___ you wrong.
man, _____ I would - n't do ___ her wrong.
man, _____ Now don't you do ___ me wrong.
man, _____ — But he's do - in' her wrong.
man, _____ — And he's do - in' you wrong.
man, _____ — But he's do - in' me wrong.
man, _____ 'Cause he was do - in' her wrong.
man, _____ She caught him do - in' her wrong.
man, _____ — But you're do - in' me wrong.
man, _____ I know I done ___ you

| C | Ab7 | G7 | **10.** C | C7 | F | F#dim | C | Db9 | C9 |

wrong. _____

1587

FAME AND FORTUNE

Words by
FRED WISE

Music by
BEN WEISMAN

Fame and for-tune, how emp-ty they can be.___ But when I hold you in my arms that's heav-en to me. Who cares for fame and for-tune? They're on-ly pass-ing things.___ But the touch of your lips on mine

FOLLOW THAT DREAM

Words by
FRED WISE

Music by
BEN WEISMAN

GOOD LUCK CHARM

Words and Music by
AARON SCHROEDER
WALLY GOLD

146-04753
1587

HARD KNOCKS

Words and Music by
JOY BYERS

142-04996
1587

HOW CAN YOU LOSE
(What You Never Had)

Words by
SID WAYNE

Music by
BEN WEISMAN

You don't have the right to cry, you be-lieved your own lie, It's your fault be-cause you thought that she was yours. Think it o-ver once, think it o-ver twice,

HEART OF ROME

Words and Music by
GEOFF STEPHENS,
ALAN BLAIKELEY and
KEN HOWARD

Moderately

Verse

In a lit - tle while you're leav - in'_____ Start - ing on the jour - ney
Sud - den - ly the tears are fall - in'_____ As we hear the whis - tle

home. Soon I'll be a - lone, the one who loves you⎫
blow. Hold me ver - y close, be - fore you leave me⎭ La, la, la, la, la,

Some - where in the Heart Of Rome.

Chorus

I'll make a wish in ev - 'ry foun - tain___ say a pray'r that you'll re - turn,

Bm A7 D Fdim A7
Minutes I'll be countin', may the fire of love still burn. I'll keep your
D G A7 F#
picture by my pillow and pretend I'm not alone.
G D A7
Make believe that you are with me, La, la, la, la, la, in the Heart Of
1. D A7
Rome.
2. D Fdim A7
Rome. I'll make a
D.S. al Fine
Fine
D A7 D A7
Rome.
Repeat and fade

HOW THE WEB WAS WOVEN

Words and Music by
CLIVE WESTLAKE and
DAVID MOST

I'M LEFT, YOU'RE RIGHT, SHE'S GONE

Words and Music by
STANLEY A. KESLER and
WILLIAM E. TAYLOR

I FORGOT TO REMEMBER TO FORGET

Words and Music by
STANLEY A. KESLER *and*
CHARLIE FEATHERS

1587

I NEED YOUR LOVE TONIGHT

Words and Music by
SID WAYNE
BIX REICHNER

146-06105
1587

need your love to-night.__ I've been wait-in' just for to-night to do some lov-in' and

hold you tight. Don't tell me, ba-by, you got-ta go;__ I got the hi - fi high and the

lights down low. Hey, now, hear what I say.__ Ooh - wow, you bet - ter stay.__ Pow -

pow, don't run a-way.__ I need your love to-night.__ Oh, __

IN YOUR ARMS

Words and Music by
AARON SCHROEDER
WALLY GOLD

I REALLY DON'T WANT TO KNOW

Words by
HOWARD BARNES

Music by
DON ROBERTSON

man-y, how man-y, I won-der? ___ But I real-ly don't want to_ know. ___ So

al-ways make me won-der; ___ Al-ways make me guess. ___ And

e-ven if I ask you, ___ Dar-ling, don't con-fess. ___ Just

let it re-main your se-cret, ___ But, dar-ling, I love you so. ___ No won-der, no

won-der I won-der, ___ Though I real-ly don't want to_ know. ___ know. ___

1587

ISLAND OF LOVE
(Kauai)

Words and Music by
**SID TEPPER
ROY C. BENNETT**

Lyrics:
Love - ly _____ prin - cess of the Is - lands. _____ Kau - a - i, _____ is - land of love. Lis - ten, _____ can't you hear her call - ing, _____ "A - lo - ha, _____ wel - come, my love."

I GOT LUCKY

Words and Music by
BEN WEISMAN
FRED WISE
DEE FULLER

I WAS THE ONE

Words and Music by
AARON SCHROEDER
CLAUDE DeMETRUIS
HAL BLAIR
BILL PEPPERS

I GOT STUNG!

Words and Music by
AARON SCHROEDER
DAVID HILL

me. It _ start-ed in my eyes, crept up to my_head. F - lew to my heart_ till_
fore. Start-ed buzz-in' in my ear, buzz-in' in my brain. Got stung all o-ver but I

I was stung dead. I'm done, uh - huh, I got stung! Mm, —
feel_ no pain.

Now, don't think I'm com - plain-in'. I'm might - y pleased we

met, 'cause you gim-me just one lit-tle peck on the back of my neck and

IT'S YOUR BABY, YOU ROCK IT

Words and Music by
SHIRL MILETE
and NORA FOWLER

142-21919
1587

broke your heart ___ and all I got to say: ___

Chorus:

It's Your Ba - by, ___ You Rock It. It's your heart - ache,

you bought it. You made ___ that bed ___ you're

sleep-in' in ___ and I'm tired ___ of hear-in' 'bout ___ it, friend, It's Your Ba-by,

I THINK I'M GONNA LIKE IT HERE

Lyrics by
DON ROBERTSON
and **HAL BLAIR**

Music by
DON ROBERTSON

146-06158
1587

140

The sound of laugh-ter from ev-'ry door - way _____

Sweet mu-sic float-ing a - cross the square; _____

It seems to say_ things are go-ing your_ way; _____ Your

trou-bles like bub-bles will soon dis-ap-pear in the air.

Down to my last pe-so,___ but I'm not a-fraid to say_ so,___ I

1587

JUST TELL HER JIM SAID HELLO

Words and Music by
JERRY LEIBER
MIKE STOLLER

142-07588
1587

International Copyright Secured
Used by permission

I SLIPPED, I STUMBLED, I FELL

Words by
FRED WISE

Music by
BEN WEISMAN

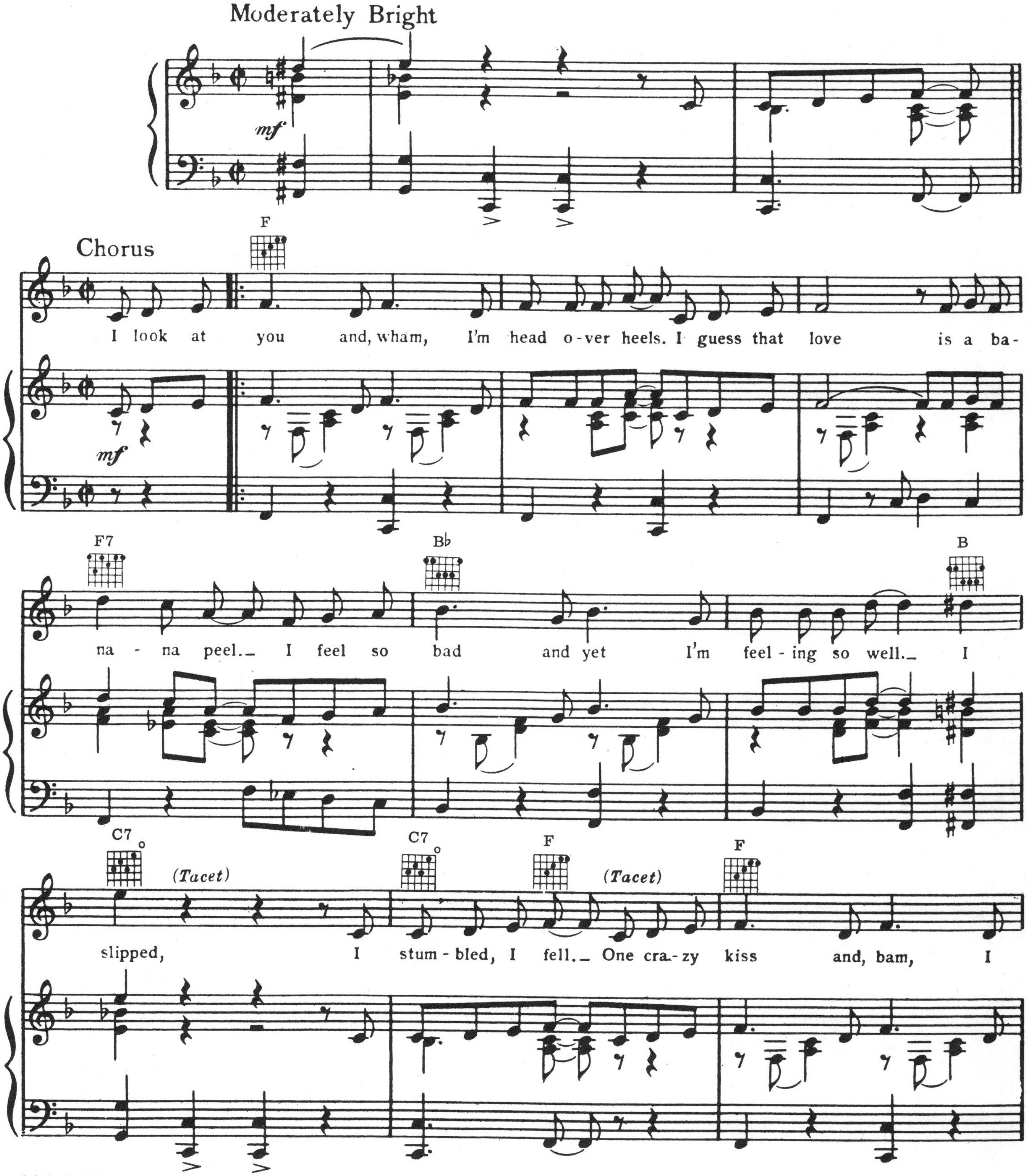

Lyrics:

I look at you and, wham, I'm head o-ver heels. I guess that love is a ba-na-na peel._ I feel so bad and yet I'm feel-ing so well._ I slipped, I stum-bled, I fell._ One cra-zy kiss and, bam, I

head for the skies. I guess that love is like a cake of ice.__ You skate a-

long, but then you nev-er can tell.__ I slipped, I

stum-bled, I fell.__ I nev-er thought I'd get tricked'-a by your sweet talk-in' lies.__

You've got a bag__ of tricks.__ And when you got bus - y I got

I'LL NEVER KNOW

Words and Music by
FRED KARGER
SID WAYNE
and **BEN WEISMAN**

KING CREOLE

Words and Music by
JERRY LEIBER
MIKE STOLLER

Bright Rock

Verse
(Tacet)

1. There's a man in New Or- leans who plays rock and roll.
2. (When the) king starts to do it, it's as good as done.
3. (Well, he) sings a song a- bout a craw- dad hole.
4. (Well, he) plays some- thing e- vil then he plays some- thing sweet.

He's a gui- tar man with a great big soul.
He holds his gui- tar like a tom- my gun.
He sings a song a- bout a jel- ly roll.
No mat- ter what he plays you got to get up on your

He lays down a beat like a ton of coal.
He starts to growl from 'way down in his throat.
He sings a song a- bout meat and greens.
feet. When he gets the rock- in' fev- er, ba- by, heav- en sakes,

142-07666
1587

He goes by the name of King Cre - ole.
He bends a string and "that's all she wrote."
He wails some blues a - bout New Or - leans.
He don't stop play - in' till the gui - tar breaks.

Chorus

You know he's gone, gone, gone, Jump - in' like a cat - fish on a pole. You know he's gone, gone, gone, Hip - shak - ing King Cre - ole.

1. 2. 3.

2. When the
3. Well, he
4. Well, he

4.

KISSIN' COUSINS

Words and Music by
FRED WISE
and **RANDY STARR**

kiss-in' cous - ins, that's what makes it all right,— all right, all right, all right. Oh,

I got a gal and she taught me how to live,— She can

give a lot and she's got a lot to give. We

kiss all night, I squeeze her tight, But we're

LET US PRAY

Words by
BUDDY KAYE

Music by
BEN WEISMAN

146-22066
1587

LONELY MAN

Words and Music by
BENNIE BENJAMIN
SOL MARCUS

146-08193
1587

1587

LONG TALL SALLY

By
ENOTRIS JOHNSON
RICHARD PENNIMAN
and ROBERT BLACKWELL

MEAN WOMAN BLUES

Words and Music by
CLAUDE DeMETRUIS

146-08722
1587

(Tacet)   (Tacet)   (Tacet)

1. A   black   cat   up   and   died   of   fright,   'Cause   she   crossed   his
2. (She)   kiss   so   hard   she   bruise   my   lips.   Hurts   so   good   my
3. (The)   strang-est gal   I   ev-   er   had;   Nev-   er   hap-   py
4. (___)   She   makes   love   with-   out   a   smile.   Ooh,   hot   dog,   that

path last night. Oh,
heart just flips. Oh,   I   got a wom-an mean as she can be.
'less she's mad. Oh,   Some-
drives me wild. Oh,

times I think she's al-most mean as me.

2. She
3. The   me.
4. ___

Some-times I think she's al-most   mean   as   me.

NEVER-ENDING

Words and Music by
BUDDY KAYE
PHILIP SPRINGER

1. Walk down to the beach at sun - set.
2. Look up at the sky at mid - night.

Look as far as you can see.
Gaze up - on the star - lit view.

You will find an end - less o - cean.
Just as heav - en has no boun - d'ries.

146-11349
1587

ONE NIGHT

Words and Music by
**DAVE BARTHOLOMEW
PEARL KING**

**CHORUS
(tacet)**

One night with you is what I'm now pray-ing for. The things that we two could plan would make my dreams come true. Just call my name and I'll be right by your side. I want your sweet help-ing hand; My love's too strong to

PARTY

Words and Music by
JESSIE MAE ROBINSON

Medium Bright Rock

Chorus

1. I feel it in my leg; I feel it in my shoe, —
2. (Some) peo-ple like to rock; some peo-ple like to roll, But
3. (I've) nev-er kissed a bear; I've nev-er kissed a goon, But
4. (Now) Honk-y Tonk-y Joe is knock-in' at the door. —

Tell me, pur-ty ba-by, if you think you feel it too.
mov-in' and a groov-in' gon-na sat-is-fy my soul.
I can shake a chick-en in the mid-dle of the room.
Bring him in and fill him up and set him on the floor.

Let's have a

146-12068
1587

PATCH IT UP

Words and Music by
EDDIE RABBITT
and RORY BOURKE

142-21725
1587

SOFTLY, AS I LEAVE YOU
(Piano)

Original Italian Text by G. Calabreste
English Lyric by
HAL SHAPER

Music by
A. DE VITA

1587

173

1587

PUPPET ON A STRING

Words and Music by
SID TEPPER and
ROY C. BENNETT

Moderately slow

Ev - 'ry time you look at me, I'm as help - less as can be;
All you do is touch my hand And your wish is my com - mand;

I be - come a pup - pet on a string And you can do 'most an - y - thing with

me.

me.

If you real - ly love me,

175

1587

PUT YOUR HAND IN THE HAND

Words and Music by
GENE MacLELLAN

Verse:

1. Ev-'ry time I look___ in-to the ho-ly book___ I wan-na trem-ble.___

When I read a-bout the part where a car-pen-ter cleared___the tem-ple___

For the buy-ers and the sell-ers were no___ dif-f'rent fel-las than what

I pro-fess___ to be.___ And it caus-es me pain___ to know I'm

not the gal that I should be.
(guy)

Put your   Put your

D.S. al Fine

1587

2. Mama taught me how to pray before I reached the age of seven.
And when I'm down on my knees that's a-when I'm close to heaven.
Daddy lived his life with two kids and a wife you do what-a you must do.
But he showed me enough of what it takes to get you through. *(Chorus)*

RELAX

Words and Music by
SID TEPPER
ROY C. BENNETT

146-13611
1587

hair down, hon - ey. Un - wind; — turn the lights down low. — Re - lax; —

— let's un - cork the stop - per. Come to Pa - pa; come

on, let's go. — De - frost — your charms; there's on - ly the two of us here. —

Come in — my arms and make your - self comf - 'ta - ble,

POOR BOY

Words and Music by
ELVIS PRESLEY and
VERA MATSON

RIDIN' THE RAINBOW

Words by
FRED WISE

Music by
BEN WEISMAN

SEPARATE WAYS

Words and Music by
RED WEST *and* **RICHARD MAINEGRA**

188

1587

SLOWLY BUT SURELY

Words by
SID WAYNE

Music by
BEN WEISMAN

STOP, LOOK, LISTEN

Words and Music by
JOY BYERS

SHAKE THAT TAMBOURINE

Words and Music by
BILL GIANT
BERNIE BAUM
and **FLORENCE KAYE**

Bright beat

142-14153
1587

SLICIN' SAND

Words and Music by
SID TEPPER
ROY C. BENNETT

Moderately bright

SO CLOSE, YET SO FAR

(From Paradise)

Words and Music by
JOY BYERS

Slowly

So close,   yet so far____ from par-a-dise,____
When you   are close to me, it's   par-a-dise,

I hold you   in my arms__ and par-a-dise____ is mine._____ Then you
We kiss,____ oh, my love,__ __ par-a-dise____ is mine. Then sud-den-ly you're

slip _____ a-way,   _____ like a child   at   play;   And
gone _____ from me,   like a float-ing star   I   see;   And

SPINOUT

Words and Music by
SID WAYNE
BEN WEISMAN *and*
DARRELL FULLER

SMORGASBORD

Words and Music by
SID TEPPER and
ROY C. BENNETT

Moderato, With a Solid Rock

Verse *Play 4 times. 4th time fade out*

1.4. Some like their wom-en short,__ some like 'em tall;__
2. Some take just ap-ple pie,__ some take just cake;__
3. Some like just south-ern belles,_ they got a one track mind;__

I'll take 'em an-y size__ 'cause I love 'em all.__
I'll take the dish I please__ and please the dish I take.__
I go for all the belles__ ex-cept the wed-ding kind.__

146-01248
1587

THE SOUND OF YOUR CRY

Words and Music by
BILL GIANT
BERNIE BAUM
FLORENCE KAYE

142-23117
1587

STARTING TODAY

Words and Music by
DON ROBERTSON

1587

214

(LET ME BE YOUR)
TEDDY BEAR

Words and Music by
KAL MANN and
BERNIE LOWE

1587

SHOUT IT OUT

Words and Music by
BILL GIANT
BERNIE BAUM
FLORENCE KAYE

Copyright © 1966 by ELVIS PRESLEY MUSIC
All rights controlled by UNICHAPPELL MUSIC, INC. (RIGHTSONG MUSIC, publisher)
Made in U.S.A.   All Rights Reserved

doubt you've a lot to shout a - bout, Give a yell, life is swell, Shout it

out.

1. Hel - lo lit - tle
2. While ___ there's good   out. _____
3. Long ___ as there's

girl, ___ don't be sad,   There's such good times   to be
food ___ you can taste,   While there's mu - sic   life's
some-one you can love,   Long as bright stars   shine a -

had;   ___ Count your   bless - ings   one by   one, ___
waste;   ___ While there's great things   hap - pen - ing, ___
bove;   You've got no   rea - son   to be   blue, ___

___ Life's a ball,   aft - er all,   have some fun. ___
___ There's no end   to the   joy   life can   bring. ___
Think what it means   when your dreams   all come   true. ___

I said, come on, get

(Tacet)   D.S. al Fine

D.S. al Fine

1587

THIS IS MY HEAVEN

Words and Music by
BILL GIANT
BERNIE BAUM
and **FLORENCE KAYE**

This is my heav - en, be - ing here with you,
You're like an an - gel sent from up a - bove,

Make it last for - ev - er;
Let's stay close to - geth - er;

This is my heav - en, it's a dream come true,
You brought me heav - en, when I shared your love,

142-15622
1587

Make it last for - ev - er._____ Come to me now and
Make it last for - ev - er._____ Here 'neath the sky be -

take my hand,_____ This is the par - a -
side the sea,_____ This is my heav - en

1.
dise I_____ planned._____

2.
when you_____ come to me._____

TODAY, TOMORROW AND FOREVER

Words and Music by
BILL GIANT
BERNIE BAUM
and **FLORENCE KAYE**

222

1587

TREAT ME NICE

Words and Music by
JERRY LEIBER *and*
MIKE STOLLER

WEAR MY RING AROUND YOUR NECK

Words and Music by
BERT CARROLL
RUSSELL MOODY

Bright Tempo

Chorus *(Tacet)*

Won't you wear my ring up a - round your neck To tell the
ring up a - round your neck To tell the

world I'm yours, by heck. Let them see
world I'm yours, by heck. Let them know

your love for me, _____ And let them see by the ring a - round your
I love you so, _____ And let them know by the ring a - round your

(Tacet)

142-16486
1587

Copyright © 1958 by ELVIS PRESLEY MUSIC and RUSH MUSIC CORP.
All rights controlled by UNICHAPPELL MUSIC, INC. (RIGHTSONG MUSIC, publisher)

1. C F C (Tacet)

neck. Won't you wear my neck.

2. C F7 C7 F7

They say that go-ing

C C7 F7

stead-y is not the prop-er thing. They say that we're too young to know the

C C7 F7 C

mean-ing of a ring. I on-ly know I love you and that you love me too.

D7 G7 D7-5 G7 (Tacet)

too. So, dar-ling, please do what I ask of you._____ Won't you wear my

1587

WE CAN MAKE THE MORNING

Words and Music by
JAY RAMSEY

WE CALL ON HIM

Words and Music by
BEN WEISMAN,
SID WAYNE and
FRED KARGER

Moderately slow, with expression

1. We call on Him when-ev-er storm clouds gath-er,
(2. We call on) Him when no one else will an-swer,

We call on Him to light our dark-est day;
We ask of Him a rea-son to go on;

Why must it be that on-ly when we're lone-ly
When our cup of joy be-comes a cup of sor-row,

146-13221
1587

WHEN I'M OVER YOU

Words and Music by
SHIRL MILETE

Lyrics:

When I'm O - ver You _____ there'll be dark-ness where my soul has been, _____ and no light_ will ev - er shine a - gain, when I'm o-ver, o - ver_ you.

When your leav - in' is

WOODEN HEART

Words and Music by
FRED WISE
BEN WEISMAN
KAY TWOMEY
BERTHOLD KAEMPFERT

YOUNG DREAMS

Words and Music by
AARON SCHROEDER
MARTIN KALMANOFF

YOU'RE THE DEVIL IN DISGUISE

Words and Music by
BILL GIANT
BERNIE BAUM
and **FLORENCE KAYE**

AIN'T THAT LOVING YOU BABY

Words and Music by
CLYDE OTIS *and*
IVORY JOE HUNTER

Medium bright blues

I __ could ride a -round the world in an old ox - cart, And nev - er let an - oth - er girl __
meet a hun - dred girls and have - uh loads of fun, My hug - gin' and my kiss - in' be -
gave me nine lives like a tom - my cat, I'd give 'em all to you and nev - er
on my Sun - day suit and I'm go - in' down - town, But I'll be kiss - in' your lips __ be - fore the

thrill __ my heart. __
longs to just one. __
take __ one back. __   Ain't that __ lov - in' you, __ ba — by?
sun __ goes down. __

Ain't that ___ lov - in' you, ___ ba - by? Ain't that ___

lov - in' you, ba - by, Ain't that lov in' you so?

1. 2, 3. C7   F7   4. C7

2. I ___ could
3. If ___ you
4. I'm put - tin'

Ain't that ___ lov - in' you, ba - by,

Ain't that lov - in' you so? ___

ROCK-A-HULA BABY

Words and Music by
FRED WISE
BEN WEISMAN
DOLORES FULLER

1. The way she moves her hips __ up to her fin-ger-tips, __ I
2. (Al - though I) love to kiss __ my lit - tle hu - la miss, __ I
3. (I bet that) she could teach __ the palms a - long the beach __ To

feel I'm heav - en bound. And when she starts to sway. __ I've
nev - er get the chance. I wan - na hold her tight __ all
sway when breez - es blow. And birds up in the sky __ could

VIVA LAS VEGAS

By
DOC POMUS *and*
MORT SHUMAN

All those hopes down the drain___ Vi _ va Las Ve-gas turn-in' day in-to

night-time, turn-in' night in-to day-time, If you see it once you'll ne-ver be the

same a-gain._____ I'm gon-na keep on the run, I'm gon-na

have me some fun if it costs me my ve-ry last dime If I wind up broke

___ well I'll al-ways re-mem-ber that I had a swing-in' time.___

CRYING IN THE CHAPEL

Words and Music by
ARTIE GLENN

251

1587

DON'T BE CRUEL
(To A Heart That's True)

Words and Music by
OTIS BLACKWELL and
ELVIS PRESLEY

1587

RETURN TO SENDER

Words and Music by
OTIS BLACKWELL
WINFIELD SCOTT

Moderately

Chorus

I gave a let-ter to the post-man; he put it in his
So then I dropped it in the mail-box_ and sent it Spe-cial

sack.
D.

Bright and ear-ly next morn-ing _ he
Bright and ear-ly next morn-ing _ it

brought my let-ter back.} She wrote up-on it: -Re-turn_ to send-er,
came right back to me.}